A Wild Silence

A Wild Silence
© John Noland, 2019

No part of this book may be reproduced by any means known at this time or derived henceforth without written permission of the publisher or author. The exception would be in the case of brief quotations embodied in the critical articles or reviews and pages where permission is specifically granted by the publisher or author.

Books may be purchased in quantity and/or special sales by contacting the publisher. All inquiries related to such matters should be addressed to:

Middle Creek Publishing & Audio
9167 Pueblo Mountain Park Road
Beulah, CO 81023
editor@middlecreekpublishing.com
(719) 369-9050

First Paperback Edition, 2019
ISBN: 978-1-7332163-9-5
Printed in the United States

Cover Art & Design: David Anthony Martin
Author photo:

A Wild Silence

John Noland

Middle Creek Publishing & Audio
Beulah, CO

ALSO BY JOHN NOLAND

This Dark Land Where I Live, Kulupi Press' 2005

The Caged and the Dying, Gribble Press, 2012

Midwestern Trees and Shadows, Finishing Line Press, 2014

That Dark and Other Light, Finishing Line Press, 2015

To Jean
with special thanks to Susan

TABLE OF CONTENTS

Spring Frogs Singing	9
The Great Blue Heron	11
Reading Deer Tracks	13
Among the White Sparrows' Calls	15
February	17
Driftwood Anchor	19
Spring Peepers	20
The Dandelion	22
An Apprentice of Sparrows	24
Oregon Winter	26
Easter Morning	27
The Whimbrel	28
The Hummingbird	29
Indian Legend Mountain	31
Red Wolves	32
Grosbeaks	33
House of Bird Songs	25
Cougar	36
Renewing the World	38
Sea Lions at Cape Arago	39
Bobwhite Quail	41
Meadowlarks	43
The Night of the Willow	45
The Other Side	47
Shorebirds Flying	49
Oregon Trees	51

Spring Frogs Singing

A bell
rings out,
another
and another,
space like the shining
of fireflies,
a tinkling
clear
as raindrops
striking dust
on a hot day.

So much
of what we are
seems by mere chance,
even those who die
and those who live,

a rhythm
almost lost
in wind
and the good darkness
of the earth,
but continual,
insistent,
one by one,

tiny bells
rising
from rain
ponds, even

puddles, one
by one

and growing
into a wave
of dark sound
passing
over the grass,

over cattails
and forsythia,

over alders
and willows

over every dark life
that glows
for a moment
inside the ringing,
awakened.

The Great Blue Heron

stands as if hacked
from blue flint. Around him
time
runs away
from
little fish
who believe
his legs
are columns
holding up
their world.
Soon
they will know
how blue lightning
strikes,
how it tears
worlds asunder.

As for the heron,
he stands
as quietly,
as innocently,
as a mystic
in contemplation
or an ancient
Japanese poet
caught
in the frozen surge
of composition
where for an instant
a haiku

will shatter
the opaque shell
of this moment,
which we call,
our world.

Reading Deer Tracks

It is like following a song
heard only
in the distance,
or like following a poem
just beginning
to be born.
It takes faith
and the certainty
that there is more
than can be seen,
the belief
that the surface
hides another world
which, if we descend
into it,
will fill us
with spirits
or at least
their words.

Almost anything
is possible, even
revelation:

this doe,
whose tracks I read, rises
as a beautiful woman
dressed in buckskins
and blue silk.
She reaches toward me,
leading me

into her world
where I become Deer

and we glide
in and out of shadows
and snow,
laced together
like poetry,
until we wander down
one last hill

and disappear
into the white
of the page–

the perfect silence
that reigns
when poems
are complete, the tracks
looking so easy,
as if this
were something we could do
everyday,
and it is

even if the deer
isn't there,
even if the snow
has melted.

Among the White Crown Sparrows' Calls

They fall, these callings,
into the blue silence
like white stones
dropped one by one,

or like red flowers
of currant bushes
shouting into brilliant
sunlight. Sometimes

I close my eyes
and they rise around me
like thick tree trunks
which hold within
themselves

whole worlds, ripe
and green
with sap, with the dance
that surges

toward stars
glittering
on crystalline nights,
or they mirror themselves--
small, brown birds
waiting to be reborn

with voices, waiting
to say, this is the way
to make a world,

this is the way
to greet
our new lives,

this is the way
to pull the earth
up through its own roots
singing and singing.

February

and cold
Here and there piebald
patches of snow

in the darkness.
It is now
the cottontail rabbits
come out.
This is the beginning

of mating season
They forget
the owl,
the coyote,

that the world
is large
and they are small.

They make
prodigious leaps,
leaps large
as they feel.

Their eyes burn
yellow
like fire in the cemetery
of their bones,
like Blake's tiger,

like the full moon

rising, telling us
we can be

unbelievably happy
in this world,
watched over
by the eyes
of stars.

Driftwood Anchor

He had found the piece of driftwood near the river when he was a boy. The year after he left home his father had made a lamp of it, and had given it to him for Christmas. Overall, it was a rather ugly scarred piece of wood. Sometimes he thought it looked more like brown bone than wood. He didn't know what he'd ever do with it–an eyesore like that. Now, thirty years later, he keeps it beside his bed. He only needs to glance at it to hear the river lapping, to see his father's eyes.

Spring Peepers

The spring peepers
have begun again
to worship
the moon
that comes up
each night
warmer
than the last.
Bright,
one-eyed,
the night
says nothing.

It does not need to.

The peepers
take care of that,
their voices
washing like a warm wave
over the darkness
haunting everything

as if the earth itself
came from a warm puddle,
moon-drunk tides
and deep
chanting

that still runs
along the spines
of those who share

this world
and know it

on the night
when wildness
celebrates
itself
with singing.

The Dandelion

The dandelion is not a question
but an answer,
a bright salute
to the sun
and the way the earth fits
and fits
every moment

while we,
who claim to love
answers,
run round
and round
asking questions

    What is it?
    What is it?

And the dandelion
whole,
complete
as a stone
goes on
filling the world
with yellow

and with seeds
blowing softly
over the earth
in answer

after answer
after answer

An Apprentice of Sparrows

Once,
at dawn,
in a winter of ice
as choirs of sparrows
caroled,
welcoming
the first vines
of brightness
into this place

I watched
and waited,
tried

to be
an apprentice
to those sparrows

who bundle
within themselves
songs of beginnings,

who believe
their joy
builds a world
note
by note.

Slowly,
so slowly,
the world,

bursting with light,
burst me
almost
into a kind
of singing–
these strange marks
on white paper
stumps
and stems
in a snowstorm,

but still rooted
in another
world.

Oregon Winter

That gray blanket
rain
hangs over everything,
breaks
into pieces,
each driving its own
faceless face
into brown grass, black mud,
gray concrete. Outside
the cat calls
to come in, and the dog
doesn't stir from the couch
where she dreams
of sunlight. Suddenly
as if the rain
were millet prayer beads
it delighted
in counting,
a song sparrow
sprinkles the morning
with bright seeds
of song–a reminder
that spring grows big
within the heavy husk
of rain.

Easter Morning

I remember coyotes
hanging upside down
on osage-orange fence posts
in the land of my childhood,
and how their howls
lit up winter evenings
with a hunger
beyond what I had known.

I hear again the wind
keening through barbed wire
as I crouch to peer
into yellow eyes
and see the brown neck hair
rise and fall. Reaching out a hand,
I stroke that fur
and know that what I touch
is a god, a voice calling
from the promised land.
And I realize there are many temples
where we worship all our lives
without even knowing.
Lost in that wild ruffle
of hair, I feel many stories.
In some you must die
to go to Heaven,
in others you must live
to save this life
that throbs around us.

The Whimbrel

The whimbrel follows
his long beak
across mudflats
probing the surface,
searching for what lies
buried. He has his own
place in this we call life.
Small enough, probably,
but he fits. The metaphor
is clear. It's not easy
being a philosopher,
sifting mud all day,
and still finding a place
to belong.

The Hummingbird

Each year it comes
initiating me again
into spring. It buzzes
over my head
in large loops, a rufous glint
of feathered light,
a spark
that might have been
struck from a flint, its voice
rattles
like a miniature bull-roarer
swung by an aborigine
calling forth mysteries
to sew up
winter wounds, the long cold
of remembering.

It flashes by
my red cap, reminding me
some days
I may be
very like a flower–quiescent,
rooted, a green hunger
rising toward a round fire
I had not even dreamed,
then bursting
into petaled, honeyed dance.

In that moment,
I am more than flesh,
and less.

Winter falls away.
A tiny ember awakens
in my knees. It flares
through me and I have to walk
into a fiery spring
where days slowly carve
the scars of belonging
in my face–
the blade,
those moments
when we
dazzle ourselves
with blooming.

Indian Legends Mountain

If on a spring day
your world has grown old
and lifeless
from too much TV,
personal sadness
or suffering,
go up on the small mountain
called, by children,
Indian Legends. Go
where salmon berries
grow. There
among the first
reddish-pink flowers
you will see
what the world
has almost forgotten–
a tiny ruby-colored bird
flashing from brown
to bright, its wings
purring
like the voice of raindrops,
its movements
like the wild dreams
of wind,
its joy
as astonishing
as the first light
reflected
in the eyes of god.

Red Wolves

They slip through shadows,
A sudden red flash, then
gone.

This is what we know,
mostly
of red wolves,
mysteries old, old
but still here,
still dying, still
shouting hosannas
and defiance
in the gold-breaking
dawn. They roam

lost to those who see
only with their eyes,
blind
to what lies hidden
in earth's dark outskirts
and in our own roiling blood
where those of us who care
pray to live wider, deep
as wolves
running wild trails
in the earth
and in our blood.

Grosbeaks

Evening grosbeaks arrive,
a raucous storm
of black and yellow
celebrating
full feeders.
Their voices croak
against the house finch's
singing, the chickadee's
calling. Like thugs,
they commandeer
the largest feeder,
squat and glare, defiant
and up to their bellies
in seeds, bullies
and proud of it.

Still, like a large drunk
at a quiet party,
they do add
a certain vigor,
a sense
that joy–
or shades of it–
still exists, though in a coarse,
rampant way.
Watching them,
I remember Army buddies–
belligerent, noisy–
some who did not
return from the jungle,
and I add

more seeds. Who knows
what fears, too
soon come true,
those uncouth calls
hide?

House of Bird Songs

Summers as a child
I lay in a huge mulberry tree
where robins, doves and sparrows
ate sun-warmed fruit,
and dreamed I could enter
the wild flight
of their singing,
understand their songs
scrolled across
the heat-dazzled sky

Now years later,
I peer into memory,
into those singing branches,
like a stranger
come home to some unknown
place, wondering why

I must always remain
an exile
from the house of bird songs,
the house of berries

where they sing stories
that still hold
my life
together.

Cougar

He comes out
of the cold country
at night, his eyes
like words hurled in war
or murmured in love,
utterances torn
from the self's marrow
as true as stone
or pain, bright
as imagined death
just before it arrives.

Nothing wild argues
against him, and only
the night knows his passing,
that slender movement
feathering the air,
teaching it a sculptured hunger.

He reaches out a paw
and caresses
those who die
for him, his hunger
a river of dream images
he has eaten and forgotten,
his great claws moving
like a chant over the land,
saying again and again

I come from the dark
to tell you

the wilderness is here,
it is everywhere,
it is in you

I come fitting
the night
like rain, fitting

us all like love,
like pain, like dream

fitting even the husk
of wild roses
blooming
just above
the green,

sharp stems.

Renewing the World

To have come to this beach, you see, is almost enough, but it needs a fire–a fire and a dream. And it needs those who know that darkness is a boat which carries us out of ourselves into the barkings of sea lions whose cries echo like whole worlds of dark birds answering an oracle, or into the gray whales' language rooted in lost cities of the sea where visions still ring with the clarity of a star. It is to sit among stones and stare into fire, seeing shapes written by wind. It is to know those shapes have meaning just outside this circle of light. It is to praise that meaning which we cannot say, a meaning strange as ourselves, and it is to enter the dream and become the fire–illuminating dark hymns of a sacred place, or to become like the tide which washes this beach as if it were cleaning an ancient, mysterious text.

Sea Lions at Cape Arago

Offshore, always offshore,
their yelping haunts the wind, cries
raw with dream and salt
so wild my blood howls
against its skin. The tide runs out
and smelt-like, I join
migrations of quick waters, leaping
from rock to black rock, questing
toward sea-lion island. Seaweed swirls
in dances of dead fingers, flares
like angel hair the sea combed,
and I see my face bright
upon the waters, drowned.
Still the call that runs beyond
runnels of the sea–lions barking
above the moon-drunk tide–carries
my feet across water-pitted stones
and gorges rushing green to open water.

I gain the island, stand on the beach, flesh
drifting in mist. Sea lions
bark at me from elephant-colored rocks, bark
stampeding toward jade waves
continuously opening. Gulls wheel
in a white fantasy of shrieking
virgins and I, an alien come home
to some unknown place, stand
like a priest in a spinning
prayer wheel surrounded by birds,
sea lions and sea–all withdrawing–

and my blood lies down in dark and salty veins
like a salmon come home
to its reflection: what else is there
than to be a quester of long calls,
a fisher of dark dreams
standing in the eye of distant cries
baying back at the green and violent sea.

Bobwhite Quail

crouch all
in a circle,
their bright eyes
watchful,
their bodies ready
to explode
into flight

that frightens
the earth,
even gives pause
to winter–
that white
and ancient hunter
who believes
in the north wind,
how it calls out
so many spirits
and takes them
to a house of ice,

but the quail know
one more verse:
how if they keep calling
and calling,
making again
their circle,
exploding
and exploding,

one day
winter, like an old
and hungry bear,
will shuffle homeward

and the spirits
he has stolen
will turn
beneath their feet
to balls of fluff

calling and calling.

This is how
we go on, they say,
listening
to the echoes
of our own voices
calling in the dark.

Meadowlarks

All day I have dreamed
in the brown, bright
meadows of their voices,
and now I see them
rise and glide
on the throb and rest
of wings,
flying toward the sun.
Around us,
daylight spills open
and the notes
of their songs
run out
like an anchor
thrown into the sea of sky.
Standing here, smiling,
I know their singing
is what holds me
to this earth, this place
of plenty where I think
there is never enough.
It is what roots me
again and again
to the depths
where my shadow
comes forth
like a quiet animal
believing it will find
the answer
to hunger
or love

while I dream
among the lost prairies
of voices
as tiny bright eyes
watch and wait
I sink down
into the grass,
willing to be one
of them, willing
to be empty
of everything
but the wild,
brown wings
of their songs.

The Night of the Willow

And a long night it is.
The willow dressed
in wedding finery,
thin leaves
like fine lace,
like a wedding gown
and its languid limbs
swaying gently
in spring's first
wind. But that does not say
what I mean. There
is a beauty, a greenness
a green feminine flame
risen from the earth,
a lightness
and an intensity
past explanation
that awakens the world.
Perhaps only the chickadees
starting to sing
among the folds
of its green
can weave the season, the saying,
the leaves
into the moment
when we see
the earth remains
more than all our fumblings,
our reasonings,
when almost overnight
the earth awakens

to green--
a singing

deep
within ourselves
deep within the world
where trees
and tiny birds
celebrate
themselves
and all of what cannot be
seen.

The Other Side

Sick, nearly, to death
of theoretical questions
and rational answers,
of getting and spending,
I wander the beach
with only stars and moon
to guide me
until I slip into mist
lighting another world
where I feel the close,
dark murmuring of shorebirds,
the dusky calling of doves,
the soft fur raccoons
keep in mystery,
and I know this place
as the crossroads with the wild
haunts me always
into deeper seeing–
a wide and awakened country
where lives are lived
beneath the same and other moon
touched by the wine
of wildness
while the slow mandala
of birds and seasons
turns and turns.

More by feel
than thought,
a knowing beyond
the rational,

I look up
into bright possibility–
the face of a white owl
hovering over me, feathers
more silent than silence
in the silver beating air.

For a moment, I almost disbelieve
what I see, but goose bumps
race up my back, and I know
more than I have ever known:
how I have been touched
by beauty from that world.

Suddenly, I see how even
the stones
of this beach burn brightly
with a dark and secret life-
stones when rubbed together
ring with inner fire-and I go on,
awakened for a moment,
into the same
and other world.

Shorebirds Flying

A river of birds
darts
dips
and wings over
the mudflats
rushing

eddying

beating back
swirling
in unison

When did we forget
to live
so perfectly?
To disappear
into each other
so completely?

And instead
to stand outside
always
knocking?

What door
did they enter
or leave,
these birds
who steer
by an inner compass,

who turn
and turn
again
as one
body?

I walk
and walk
on the beach,
trying to find
such wild country

at my own center
where,
with love
and letting go,

I might fly!

Oregon Trees

People ask why
I stay here
on this green and empty edge
of a continent.
I try to explain
how it is to live listening
to the ecstatic calls
of sea lions
telling dark stories
while the restless sea
adds its rhythm
to the night;
how off-shore
on huge basalt rocks
black oystercatchers
add the wheep! wheep!
of their cries
to this cacophony
of wildness,
throbbing and dancing
but rooted as bull kelp
to this place
where sea
and land meet.
I try to tell how it speaks
of a wild hunger
running through limb
after limb
of fir, spruce, cedar,
myrtle,
and how I hunker down

on dark nights
listening
to the rasp
of branch
on branch
until finally
I go out, spread fingers
on a trunk
and know for a moment
on this day,
in this place,
I can still touch
the green fire
that goes beyond
the merely human.

Acknowledgments

The following poems have been previously published in the following publications.

"Among the White Sparrow's Calls"	*Albatross*
"Coastal Oregon "	*The Avocet*
"House Finches"	*Intricate Homeland*
	Timberline Review
"Meadowlarks"	*Big Muddy, Vol. 51*
"Oregon Trees" *Echoes*	*Rogue River*
	Windfall
"Renewing the World"	*Seattle Review*
"River Breaks"	*The Avocet*

ABOUT THE AUTHOR

John Noland lives and writes near the ocean in Coos Bay, Oregon. He has published in Chicago Review, Orion, Nature Writing 1999 ed. by John Murray, Georgetown Review, Seattle Review, Laurel Review, Poet Lore, Limestone, Big Muddy, Camas, Intricate Homelands, and other journals. His chapbook, This Dark Land Where I Live, won Kulupi Press' 2005 Poems of Place contest. The Caged and the Dying, won the Gribble Press 2012 Chapbook contest. In 2014 Midwestern Trees and Shadows was published by Finishing Line Press and That Dark and Other Light in 2015.

Middle Creek Publishing Titles

Span   David Anthony Martin

Deepening the Map   David Anthony Martin

Phases   Erika Moss Gordon

Cirque & Sky   Kathleen Willard

Messiah Complex and Other Stories   Michael Olin-Hitt

Lessons from Fighting The Black Snake at Standing Rock
Nick Jaina and Leslie Orihel

Wild Be   One Leaf

Bijoux   David A. Martin

Sawhorse   Tony Burfield

Almost Everything, Almost Nothing   KB Ballentine

Kimono Mountain   Mike Parker

p a l e o s   Hoag Holmgren

I   Bengt O Björklund

Across the Light   Bruce Owens

Faces of Fishing Creek   Kyle Laws

No Better Place: A New Zen Primer   Hoag Holmgren

a daughters aubade (sailing out from Sognefjord)   Mara Adamitz Scrupe

Unraveling the Endless Knot   Sandra Noel

The Shaman Speaks Joseph Murphy

Sphinx   Andrea Dejean

Secondary Cicatrices   Lynne Goldsmith

ABOUT MIDDLE CREEK PUBLISHING

MIDDLE CREEK PUBLISHING believes that responding to the world through art & literature — and sharing that response — is a vital part of being an artist.

MIDDLE CREEK PUBLISHING is a company seeking to make the world a better place through both the means and ends of publishing. We are publishers of quality literature in any genre from authors and artists, both seasoned and as-yet undervalued, with a great interest in works which may be considered to be, illuminate or embody any aspect of contemplative Human Ecology, defined as the relationship between humans and their natural, social, and built environments.

MIDDLE CREEK's particular interest in Human Ecology, is meant to clarify an aspect of the quality in the works we will consider for publication and is meant as a guide to those considering submitting work to us. Our interest is in publishing works illuminating the Human experience through words, story or other content that connects us to each other, our environment, our history and our potential deeply and more consciously.

www.ingramcontent.com/pod-product-compliance
Lightning Source LLC
Chambersburg PA
CBHW022121090426
42743CB00008B/955